SUPER SMART
INFORMATION
STRATEGIES

UNDERSTANDING AND CREATING INFOGRAPHICS

FOSSIL RIDGE PUBLIC LIBRARY DISTRICT
BRAIDWOOD, IL 60408

by Kristin Fontichiaro

CHERRY LAKE PUBLISHING • ANN ARBOR, MICHIGAN

CHERRY LAKE
Publishing

A NOTE TO PARENTS AND TEACHERS: Please remind your children how to stay safe online before they do the activities in this book.

A NOTE TO KIDS: Always remember your safety comes first!

Published in the United States of America
by Cherry Lake Publishing
Ann Arbor, Michigan
www.cherrylakepublishing.com

Content Adviser: Gail Dickinson, PhD, Associate Professor,
Old Dominion University, Norfolk, Virginia

Photo Credits: Cover, ©The Department for Culture, Media and Sport / www.flickr.com / CC-BY-2.0; page 4, ©Hey Paul / www.flickr.com / CC-BY-2.0; page 8, ©Samuel Borges Photography/Shutterstock, Inc.; page 9, ©I Bike Fresno / www.flickr.com / CC-BY-2.0; page 10, ©iStockphoto.com/gisele; page 11, ©iStockphoto.com/william87; page 12, ©Monkey Business Images/Dreamstime.com; page 14, ©eZeePics Studio/Shutterstock, Inc.; page 16, ©Elnur/Shutterstock, Inc.; page 18, ©Waag Society / www.flickr.com / CC-BY-2.0; page 20, ©Aprescindere/Dreamstime.com; page 21, ©Olesya Feketa/Shutterstock, Inc.; page 22, ©iStockphoto.com/nicolamargaret; page 24, ©Gelpi JM/Shutterstock, Inc.; page 26, ©Lucky Business/Shutterstock, Inc.; page 28, ©Yodel Anecdotal / www.flickr.com / CC-BY-2.0

Library of Congress Cataloging-in-Publication Data
Fontichiaro, Kristin.
  Understanding and creating infographics / by Kristin Fontichiaro.
       pages cm. — (Information explorer)
  Includes bibliographical references and index.
  ISBN 978-1-62431-126-0 (lib. bdg.) — ISBN 978-1-62431-258-8 (pbk.) — ISBN 978-1-62431-192-5 (e-book)
  1. Visual communication—Juvenile literature. 2. Charts, diagrams, etc.—Juvenile literature. I. Title.

  P93.5.F66 2014   2013014828
  302.2'2—dc23

Cherry Lake Publishing would like to acknowledge the work of The Partnership for 21st Century Skills. Please visit www.p21.org for more information.

Printed in the United States of America
Corporate Graphics Inc.
July 2013
CLFA13

Table of Contents

CHAPTER ONE
What Is an Infographic?

Infographics along our roads help keep us safe. →

Our world is full of words: homework assignments, text messages, Web pages, and books. It is also full of useful numbers: speed limit signs, clocks, and thermometers all communicate important information about the world. And have you ever heard someone say, "a picture is worth a thousand words"? This means that images such as photographs, drawings, or maps can sometimes communicate more than words or numbers can. When you combine words, numbers, and images, you can create a powerful document that presents a large amount of information in a small amount of space.

An infographic is a document that combines words, numbers, and images to explain something in an appealing visual way. Infographics can be used to inform, **persuade**, or raise questions. Sometimes they are also used to advertise products. You can find them in places such as newspapers, magazines, and Web sites. They're a fun way to learn new things and a fun way to share what you've learned, too!

Have you ever made mind maps at school? These quick sketches show how your ideas are connected to each other. At school, you might also sometimes fill in worksheets called graphic organizers, where the spaces are planned out for you in advance. Are mind maps and graphic organizers infographics? Well, not exactly. They have words arranged visually, and they help you plan your work, but they can be hard for someone else to read and understand. Infographics are different because they

- are made up of small bits of information that, together, communicate a big idea;
- are finished work, rather than just quick notes;
- are organized clearly so the information is presented in order;
- are easy to understand;
- are designed to look good, with **fonts**, images, colors, and shapes that are carefully selected to work together.

TRY THIS!

Educator David Warlick collects interesting infographics. You can browse recent posts at http://davidwarlick.com/graphicaday until you find a topic that interests you. At first, you'll see a tiny version of the infographic, known as a thumbnail. Click on the thumbnail to reveal a larger version of the graphic. Some infographics are so wide or tall that they must be shrunk to fit on the screen. Your cursor may turn into a magnifying glass with a "+" inside. That means that you can click on the image to zoom in and see the infographic in greater detail.

Continued on the next page

With a friend, find at least three infographics. Ask yourselves these questions:

- What is the purpose of this infographic? Is it to inform, persuade, raise questions, or advertise? Which parts of the infographic give you that information?

Purpose?

Message?

- What is the infographic's main message?
- Where do you see charts or graphs that turn numbers into pictures? How do they help you understand the numbers?
- What types of images are used? Photographs? **Icons**? Cartoons? Original artwork?

- In what order should you read the information? Top to bottom? Left to right? Clockwise? Are there arrows or lines that help you figure this out?
- Who created the infographic?
- Where did they find their information? (Look for **citations** of books or Web pages at the bottom of the infographic.)

CHAPTER TWO
Reading Infographics

You can zoom in on parts of an infographic when viewing it online.

Infographics are often designed to be much bigger than the pages of a book or the shape of a computer monitor. This means they can include a lot of information. What's the best way to tackle a huge infographic? It might seem like you should start at the top or in the upper left-hand corner, just like you do with a book. However, you might want to put on your detective hat before you do that.

Newspapers and magazines create infographics to quickly and easily share information with readers. The infographics found in trustworthy newspapers and magazines—whether in the print versions or online—have an **objective** point of view. They should not display the creator's **bias**. That means they focus on facts, not opinions.

Many other organizations and companies make infographics to convince readers to take a certain position on an issue or buy a product. Although these infographics may be full of facts, the creators have carefully picked the facts that best support their goal. That means that there can be a strong bias. You might not be getting all of the information about a topic. You

Some infographics try to convince readers to do an activity, such as ride a bicycle.

Checking out an infographic's creator and sources helps you figure out its purpose.

might be getting just the information that matches the creator's point of view.

Individuals and companies put their names (and possibly their logos) at the bottom of the infographics they create. Checking the bottom of an infographic and figuring out who made it should be your first step when looking at one of these documents. Knowing something about the author can help you figure out if you are being informed or persuaded.

The second thing to check at the bottom of the page is the list of information sources (such as books, Web sites, or articles) that the creator used to make the infographic. Do those resources seem like they are trustworthy?

The bottom of an infographic might also have **copyright** information. Infographics are owned by the people who created them. You should avoid copying and sharing copyrighted work with others unless you have permission from the copyright holder.

However, some infographic designers want you to copy and share their work. When you look at an infographic, you might see a reference to Creative Commons or an icon like the one below. Creators can use Creative Commons licenses to signal the ways others are allowed to share, reuse, or edit their work. To figure out what different Creative Commons licenses allow you to do, visit *http://creativecommons.org/licenses*.

Web sites such as Flickr allow users to search for and share Creative Commons images.

↰ Take notes on your ideas as you study various infographics.

Now you know who made the infographic, where they got their information, and the ways in which you can share what they made. That means it is time to take a look at the infographic itself.

Some infographics you find online are tall and narrow. You might have to scroll down to see the whole thing. Try reading these infographics from top to bottom. Other infographics are wide instead of tall. This means they are meant to be read from left to right. Some infographics put information in a circular or wheel shape. Try reading them in a clockwise direction.

As you read, ask yourself the following questions:

- What does this mean?
- What am I supposed to learn from reading this?
- How does this information work together?

TRY THIS!

You have just found an awesome new infographic. Because you are a smart searcher, you check the bottom information before you start reading. Look at the creators' names below. Which ones are likely to be objective and without bias? Which might be designed to persuade you or sell you something? Which ones might require you to read the entire infographic before you can be sure?

1. The United States Department of Commerce
2. Harvard University
3. Joe Smith
4. Jones Computer Company
5. The Committee to Prevent Smoking

Knowing who created the infographic helps me figure out its purpose.

To get a copy of this activity, visit www.cherrylakepublishing.com/activities.

ANSWERS:
#1 and #2 are most likely objective because one is a government source and one is a university.
#3 was written by a person who is not associated with a trusted group. We don't know who he is or what he believes, so we have to read the infographic before deciding.
#4 is from a company, so it is possible that it intends to sell a product or service. You will have to read the infographic to be sure.
#5 is probably persuasive. We can guess that the infographic might have information that persuades you not to smoke.

CHAPTER THREE

Gathering Information

You will need to gather plenty of information to make an infographic on dolphins.

Reading infographics is a cool way to take in information. It is also fun to make infographics of your own. Well-designed, well-researched infographics help you communicate the things you've learned.

Begin your research by considering a topic or theme. For example, maybe you are interested in dolphins. First, you need to get some basic information about these animals. You'll want to know where they live, what they eat, and which animals eat them. Talk with your teacher and librarian about books, databases, and Web sites that will help you learn the basics.

As you discover good information, start making notes. You don't need to copy whole sentences. Try to put things in your own words and use the fewest number of words possible.

One cool strategy is to get a manila file folder and a stack of sticky notes in different colors. Put one piece of information on each sticky note. Use different colored sticky notes for each Web site or book, so you can quickly tell which information came from which source. Make one sticky note for each color that tells you the source of the information (include the author, title, and URL) so you don't forget. Store your completed sticky notes in the manila file folder so they don't get lost.

Now that you know some basic information about your subject, sort through your sticky notes. Do your notes lead you to any new questions? For example, you might have read that dolphins like to do tricks. That might inspire you to ask questions like:

- How do people learn to become dolphin trainers?
- How long does it take a dolphin to learn a new trick?
- How often do dolphins make mistakes when they are asked to do a trick?
- What kinds of rewards do dolphins receive for doing tricks?

You might want to use different colors of sticky notes for the different sources you use.

Next, do another round of research to try to track down answers to these new questions. Keep adding to your collection of sticky notes, remembering to change colors for each new source. Keep an eye open for numbers and **statistics**, because those are powerful ways to communicate information in an infographic.

How do you know when you're done researching? That is a tough question. After all, some people study dolphins their entire lives. Open your folder and rearrange your notes. Group similar pieces of information together. For example, you might place all of the information you have about baby dolphins together. Are there holes in your information? Ask yourself, "What is the story that these notes are telling me? What is the big idea that people will understand about dolphins based on these notes?" When you can answer those questions, you are probably ready to move on to the next step!

To get a copy of this activity, visit www.cherrylakepublishing.com/activities.

TRY THIS!

Imagine that you have been researching the duck-billed platypus. Here is some basic information that you have found. Notice how these notes save space by using symbols, abbreviations, and only the most important words. What additional research questions can you think of after reading these facts?

- Platypus = mammal = warm-blooded
- Most mammals have live babies. Platypus has eggs!
- Home = Australia
- Mouth shaped like duck's bill (but not a bird's beak)
- Webbed feet
- NOT a bird

CHAPTER FOUR
Organizing Your Content

A storyboard is a way to organize your ideas visually before starting the final project.

By this point, you are probably itching to open up a computer program or online tool and start making your own infographic. Hold on a minute! Did you know that professional moviemakers and comic book artists make a plan before they start making stuff? It's true! They often use a **storyboard** to help them organize their ideas quickly. In a storyboard, they sketch out the major ideas of their movie or comic. Storyboards are like visual outlines of what will happen in the finished project. They show only the important parts of a project and often leave out smaller details.

The hardest part of making an infographic is organizing your ideas, so follow the professionals' advice and make a plan first. Think back to when you were first collecting sticky notes. Were they in any order or sequence? No! They were just ideas scattered inside your folder.

Great infographics have a secret: the ideas and numbers in them have been carefully selected and organized so that they flow naturally from one idea to the next. The process of organizing information in a way that appeals to both the eye and the mind is known as information visualization. When you decide on the message you want people to receive and then organize the information to match the message, you're communicating powerfully.

Information visualization can be just as tricky for adults as it is for kids! An architect named Richard Saul Wurman was interested in how he could organize information, just as he had organized parts of a building. He designed the LATCH (Location, Alphabet, Time, Category, Hierarchy) system for **categorizing** items. This system offers five ways to sort information visually:

1. **L**ocation: Have you ever used a map to help you travel somewhere new? Then you have seen information organized by location. You can estimate

how far things are from one another by their
distance on the map. Green areas indicate parks or
forests, while blue areas indicate water. A larger font
size indicates larger cities. Wider lines mean bigger
roads and highways. A dolphin infographic organized
by location might sort dolphin information by
place. All of the information about amusement park
dolphins would go in one area of the infographic,
and all of the information about dolphins that live in
the ocean would go in another.

On maps, cities written in smaller letters
have smaller populations, and larger cities are
written in bigger or bolded letters.

If your teacher assigns seats at school, you and your classmates might sit in alphabetical order.

2. **A**lphabet: In school, your teachers might use seating charts or line up students to go to lunch. In these situations, people are often sorted alphabetically. If you have ever read an animal alphabet book, in which there is one animal for each letter of the alphabet, then you've seen information organized alphabetically. If you wanted to organize your dolphin infographic alphabetically, you could write each letter of the alphabet in a line on the left side of your infographic and then give a fact that corresponds to each letter.

3. **T**ime: How do you know what to do at what time when you are at school? There is probably a schedule

Recipes organize cooking steps by time. Imagine what would happen if a recipe told you to frost a cake before baking it!

and a calendar in the room. These are ways of organizing your life according to time. Some books include timelines where events are organized in order from the earliest to the latest. You see timelines in many history or social studies books. Other ways to organize information by time include recipes and model kit instructions. These are organized from the first step to the last. You could organize your dolphin infographic by time by detailing a dolphin's life cycle. Put all the information about infancy at the beginning, then talk about how a dolphin grows, and then detail its adulthood.

4. **C**ategory: When you go to the grocery store, do you find one brand of butter next to the broccoli and another next to the muffins? No! All of the butter products are near one another in the refrigerated case. And because butter is a dairy product, you can find it near other dairy products, such as yogurt, milk, and cheese. A grocery store is a great example of items that are organized by category. If you wanted to organize a dolphin infographic by category, you would put similar information together. For example, all of your research about dolphin habitats could go in one section, and all of the information about dolphin tricks could go in another area.

5. **H**ierarchy: When people sort by hierarchy, they sort from the most to the least or from the least to the most. In a school hierarchy, the superintendent is at the top. Next is the principal, and then the teacher. In a hierarchy of shapes, you might move from a triangle (three sides) to a square (four sides) to a pentagon (five sides) to a hexagon (six sides). You can also use a hierarchy to sort by numbers. For example, a pet hierarchy might list the person with the most pets first, down to the person with the fewest pets. Creating a dolphin infographic by hierarchy would be tricky and might not work very well!

You might organize an infographic on training dolphins by time (which skills are learned first) or by hierarchy (which skills are the most important).

Before you begin organizing your notes, write your infographic's title on the top of your folder. What's the main idea you want people to come away with? It could be:

- Save the Dolphins! (persuasive)
- Dolphins: Friendly Mammals (informational)
- How Dolphins Learn Tricks (informational)

Now take some time to rearrange the sticky notes in your folder. Which of the LATCH techniques might help you best communicate your message? Try sorting your information in a couple of different ways. (If you're worried that you'll forget what you did, take a photo before you rearrange your notes again.) Don't be afraid to discard notes that don't fit with your message. Remember, you want your facts to tell a story!

TRY THIS!

To learn more about the LATCH system and see examples of LATCH in action, watch the animated video at http://bit.ly/learn-latch Then talk about these questions with a friend:

1. How would you organize information about your topic by time? By category? What kinds of information would you need to collect for each method of organization?

2. What would it look like if you organized information about your favorite sports team alphabetically? By location? Which kinds of information would you need for each?

3. How would you organize your family by hierarchy? Would your little sister, big brother, aunt, or grandparent agree with your system?

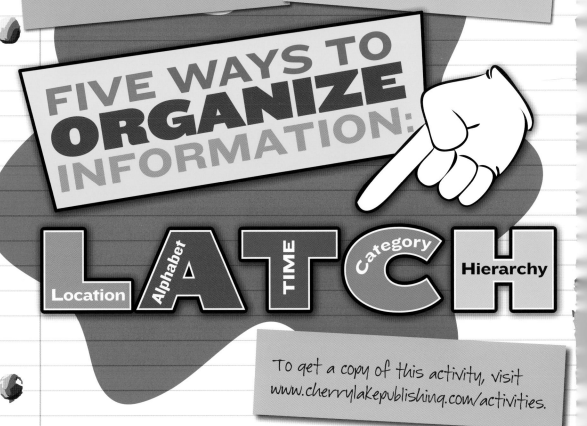

FIVE WAYS TO ORGANIZE INFORMATION:

LATCH

Location Alphabet TIME Category Hierarchy

To get a copy of this activity, visit www.cherrylakepublishing.com/activities.

CHAPTER FIVE
Designing Your Infographic

It might be easiest for you to make your infographic on a computer.

You've collected your information and sketched out the order and flow of your ideas. You feel confident that you have more than a random bunch of facts. You've got data that tells a story. Now it's time for the most creative part: designing your infographic!

While you can draw your infographic by hand, most designers use computer software. At your home, library, or school, you probably have slideshow software, such as

Microsoft PowerPoint or Apple Keynote. You can design your infographic on a slide by using the software's clip art and typing tools. You can also experiment with a tool made just for creating infographics. Try one of these:

- Visually (*http://visual.ly*)
- Easelly (*http://easel.ly*)
- IBM Many Eyes (*http://www-958.ibm.com/ software/analytics/manyeyes*)

Remember your file folder full of sorted and sequenced sticky notes? That's your visual outline. Now you can transfer that outline to a digital tool and turn your notes into a colorful infographic! Infographics use colors, images, charts and graphs, numbers, words, and arrows to communicate ideas. Let's talk about each one.

Choose *colors* that work well together. If you are making a dolphin infographic, you might choose to use blues (for water) and grays (for the animals). If you were making an infographic about the U.S. government, you might use a lot of red, white, and blue.

Use *images* to draw the reader's eye toward important ideas. Professionals use just one kind of image at a time, so either choose all photographs, all colorful clip art drawn in a similar style, or all black-and-white art. Creative Commons images are graphics that the artist wants you to use (instead of just copying any graphic you find from the Web), so try starting your image search at *http://search.creativecommons. org*. Visit *http://thenounproject.com* for strong black-and-white images that are licensed under Creative Commons. Their simple shapes and bold lines make them a great option.

Use *charts* and *graphs* when you want to compare two sets of numbers. For example, if you want to compare the length of a baby dolphin to the length of its mother, a graph can help people quickly see the difference.

Use *numbers* to make a statistic stand out. For example, some dolphins have up to 250 teeth! Make the number 250 really big to stand out and draw attention.

Notice how this infographic uses purple, pink, blue, and green throughout. This creates a pleasing look.

TRY THIS!

Browse the online infographic tools described in this chapter. Which would you use if you were making an infographic about the life cycle of a dolphin? How would you decide?

To get a copy of this activity, visit www.cherrylakepublishing.com/activities.

Use *words* to communicate facts that can't be expressed in any other way. Use very few words so they don't clutter the overall image.

Use *arrows* if needed to indicate the sequence in which someone should take in the information.

You're almost done, but don't forget the information that goes at the bottom of your infographic: your name as the creator; a list of the books, Web sites, and images you used to find information; and whether the work is copyrighted (and nobody else can share or reuse it without your permission) or shared with a Creative Commons license (in which you give permission in advance for your work to be shared or reused under the conditions you identify).

Congratulations! You're well on your way to becoming an information visualization expert!

Glossary

bias (BYE-uhs) a point of view that favors one side of an argument

categorizing (KAT-uh-guh-rize-ing) grouping things together based on their characteristics

citations (sy-TAY-shuhnz) descriptions of sources used to provide information for a project

copyright (KAH-pee-rite) the legal right to control the use of something created, such as a song, book, or picture

fonts (FAHNTS) styles of type

icons (EYE-kahnz) graphic symbols on a computer screen representing programs, functions, or files

objective (uhb-JEK-tiv) based on facts, instead of opinions or feelings; fair

persuade (pur-SWADE) to make someone do or believe something by giving the person good reasons

statistics (stuh-TIS-tiks) numerical information

storyboard (STOR-ee-bord) a way of visually outlining the story of a movie or comic book

Find Out More

BOOKS

Fontichiaro, Kristin, and Emily Johnson. *Know What to Ask:
Forming Great Research Questions.* Ann Arbor, MI.: Cherry
Lake, 2012.

Rabbat, Suzy. *Using Digital Images.* Ann Arbor, MI.: Cherry
Lake, 2011.

Robinson, Craig. *Flip Flop Fly Ball: An Infographic Baseball
Adventure.* New York: Bloomsbury, 2011.

WEB SITES

Kathy Schrock's Guide to Everything: Infographics

www.schrockguide.net/infographics-as-an-assessment.html

This site has great tips for creating infographics, tools to make
them, and other helpful resources.

What Is an Infographic?

http://visual.ly/what-is-an-infographic

Find a definition of infographics on this Web site for infographics creation.

Index

About the Author

Kristin Fontichiaro teaches at the University of Michigan. She has written many books for students and adults.